101 Coolest Things Do in Canada

© 2017 101 Coolest Things

All rights reserved. No part of this publication may be reproduced, distributed, or transmitted in any form or by any means, including photocopying, recording, or other electronic or mechanical methods, without the prior written permission of the publisher, except in the case of brief quotations embodied in critical reviews and certain other noncommercial uses permitted by copyright law.

Introduction

So you're going to Canada, huh? You lucky lucky thing! You are sure in for a treat because Canada is a huge place that offers tonnes to explore, whether you're obsessed with nature, you're a culture vulture, or you just fancy eating in some great restaurants.

This guide will take you on a journey from the major cities like Toronto, Montreal, and Vancouver, and through to national parks, islands, and the Canadian Rockies.

In this guide, we'll be giving you the low down on:
- the very best things to shove in your pie hole, from comfort food like poutine, through to the best seafood restaurants in the country
- incredible festivals, whether you would like to party hard to international bands or you would like to watch film projections on the walls of a snow castle
- the coolest historical and cultural sights that you simply cannot afford to miss from the city walls of

Quebec through to world-class art galleries across the country

- the most incredible outdoor adventures, whether you want to have a white water rafting adventure in the Rockies, or you fancy going on a dog sledding ride

- the places where you can party like a local and make new friends

- and tonnes more coolness besides!

Let's not waste any more time – here are the 101 coolest things not to miss in Canada!

1. Conquer a Fear of Heights at CN Tower's Glass Floor

Toronto is a great looking city, but you can only get a limited sense of it when you walk along Toronto's streets. To get a better view, you need to check out the observation decks from the CN Tower, which was the world's tallest tower at the time of being built in 1976. For an experience you won't forget in a hurry, head up to the Glass Floor. As you might have guessed, the floor is completely made of glass, and as it's located 342 metres above the ground, so looking down can take all of your nerve.

(301 Front St W, Toronto, ON M5V 2T6, www.cntower.ca)

2. Watch the Summer Polar Bears of Churchill

Churchill is a small town in the Hudson Bay area of the Manitoba state, but although it's a small town, it attracts a decent amount of tourists each year because this is the place you need to be if you would like to see polar bears in person. This part of the world has the most accessible polar bear population on the planet, and there are plenty of tour companies that can take you into the natural habitat of the polar bear so that you can see them as they actually live.

3. Find Peace at Dr. Sun-Yat Sen Classical Chinese Garden

Vancouver is often considered to be the most attractive city in Canada, and that is partly because of the very many peaceful green spaces that are dotted in and around the city. Dr. Sun-Yat Sen Classical Chinese Garden is one of the most unique and special of these places. Built to maintain the understanding between Chinese and Western cultures, the park contains a large pond with fish, craggy rocks, and greenery to combine all the elements of nature in one garden.

(578 Carrall St, Vancouver, BC V6B 5K2, http://vancouverchinesegarden.com/)

4. Have a Day of Learning at the Royal Ontario Museum

The Royal Ontario Museum is a place where you can spend days and days, so expansive are the exhibitions that cover art, world culture, and natural history. With a collection size of more than 6 million objects, this is one of the largest museums in all of North America. Among the collections, you can find dinosaurs, minerals and meteorites, couture clothing, product design objects, and African art.

(100 Queens Park, Toronto, ON M5S 2C6, www.rom.on.ca/en)

5. Enjoy the Fun of the Rodeo at Calgary Stampede

If you are a fun seeker through and through, it doesn't get much more fun and entertaining than the Calgary Stampede, a rodeo, exhibition, and festival that is hosted in Calgary every July. The ten day festival is billed as the greatest show on earth, and in our opinion that's really not much of an exaggeration. Of course, you can experience live rodeo events, but you can also take in music concerts, stage shows, parades, agricultural competitions, and loads more.

(1410 Olympic Way SE, Calgary, AB T2G 2W1, www.calgarystampede.com)

6. Tuck Into a Big Plate of Poutine

Canada might not be one of the first places that springs to mind when you think of foodie destinations around the world, but there is a handful of dishes native to Canada that every food lover should try, and perhaps the best known of these is poutine. Originating from Quebec, this dish is French fries that are topped with cheese curds and a light brown gravy. This is the basic version, but you can also choose toppings like sausage, chicken, and bacon if you're a meat lover.

7. Be Stunned by the Cathedral-Basilica of Notre-Dame de Quebec

Without a doubt, one of the most awe inspiring churches in all of Canada is the Cathedral-Basilica of Notre-Dame de Quebec, which you will find in beautiful Quebec City. This cathedral has been on the same spot since the mid 17th century, and many important figures from the history of Quebec, and indeed Canada, are buried here. The stained glass windows are especially beautiful.

(16 Rue De Buade, Ville de Québec, QC G1R 4A1, www.notre-dame-de-quebec.org)

8. Get Sporty at the Hockey Hall of Fame

Ice hockey is the national winter sport of Canada, and any sports lover should get to grips with this sport on a trip to the country. The Hockey Hall of Fame in Toronto is the ideal spot to do exactly that. But this is more than just a place where you'll see hockey player's names written on plaques on the wall – it's a dynamic and innovative place to learn about hockey. Inside you'll find a replica NHL dressing room, hockey artefacts from all over the world, and hi-tech games that challenge your goalkeeping and shooting skills.

(30 Yonge St, Toronto, ON M5E 1X8, www.hhof.com)

9. Watch International Bands at Osheaga

If you can't get enough of summer festivals, you might be wondering which parties you can attend across Canada this summer. Well, Osheaga is one of the most popular of them all, even if you haven't heard of it before. This multi-day indie festival is hosted in Montreal, and normally at the end of July. This festival attracts world class talents, and some of the acts that have performed in the past are Arcade Fire, Coldplay, The Killers, and Lana del Rey.

(www.osheaga.com)

10. Climb Point Prim Lighthouse for a Spectacular View

Prince Edward Island is the only island province of Canada, which makes it a great place to get away from it all, and enjoy the landscapes and tranquillity. One of the most visited spots on the island is Point Prim Lighthouse, one of only two circular lighthouses that can be found in all of Canada. In the summer months, it's possible to climb to the top of the lighthouse tower, and enjoy the spectacular views over the ocean.

(2147 Point Prim Rd, Belfast, PE C0A 1A0, www.pointprimlighthouse.com)

11. Learn Something New at the Canadian Museum of Immigration

Canada has a long tradition of welcoming people from other countries into the nation, and providing them with a place to live, work, and raise their families. The best place to learn about this incredible tradition of hospitality is at the Canadian Museum of Immigration in Halifax, Nova Scotia. The museum is located on a pier and it informs visitors about what it was like to arrive at this pier as an immigrant from 1928 – 1971, about the lives of those people, and how they have contributed to Canada.

(1055 Marginal Rd, Halifax, NS B3H 4P7, www.pier21.ca/home)

12. Get Close to Sea Life at Ripley's Aquarium of Canada

Since Canada is a country with a great deal of coastline, the waters are extremely rich with marine life, and if you visit the Ripley's Aquarium of Canada in Toronto you won't even need to get your feet wet to get up close to it. With around 13,500 beautiful sea creatures, there is always plenty to see. Some of the more unique species you will find in the aquarium are the upside-down jelly, whitespotted bamboo sharks, and unicorn surgeonfish.

(288 Bremner Blvd, Toronto, ON M5V 3L9, www.ripleyaquariums.com/canada)

13. Stroll the Breath Taking Glacier Skywalk

Inside the Jasper National Park in the Rockies, you can find something that is truly breath taking: the Glacier Skywalk. This observation walk takes you on a cliff edge walkway with a glass bottomed path, giving you panoramic views of all the beauty of the Rockies. All around you, will experience the most stunning alpine and glacial vistas, including waterfalls that gush with power like you have never seen before.

(Icefields Pkwy, Banff, AB T0E 1E0, www.brewster.ca/attractions-sightseeing/glacier-skywalk/)

14. Feel Artsy at the Museum of Contemporary Canadian Art

Canada is a country that is full of creativity and you can feel the heartbeat of this creativity at the Museum of Contemporary Canadian Art in Toronto. This isn't a huge gallery but it's one of the most dynamic and forward thinking cultural spaces that you are likely to enter in Canada. They are committed to promoting the work of local artists with a selection of permanent and temporary exhibits. Arts lovers could easily spend a whole afternoon walking around.

(80 Ward St #199, Toronto, ON M6H 4A6, http://museumofcontemporaryart.ca)

15. Enjoy Winter Activities at Fete des Neiges

Canada is one of those destinations that offers something very different across all seasons of the year, and in the winter time, we think there's no better way to experience all the Canadian cold has to offer than at Fete des Neiges, otherwise known as the Montreal Snow Festival. The festival is held each year from January to early February, and features an ice sculpture playground, hockey tournaments, tubing, snowshoeing, skating, and lots more wintry fun.

16. Play Some Volleyball on English Bay Beach

Located along the coastline of Vancouver, the English Bay Beach is one of the sandy gems of this city. Although it's located in the city, it's a 30 minute walk from other beaches in the downtown area which means that it's far less developed and you certainly won't be jostling for towel space. But what we really love about English Bay Beach are the two large sand volleyball courts so that you can get active in the Vancouver sunshine if you so wish.

17. Join in With the Fun of Canada Day in Ottawa

Canada Day lands on July 1st each year, and it exists to commemorate the enactment of the Constitution Act of 1867, which united the three separate provinces of Canada to become one nation. Since Ottawa is the capital city, this is the perfect place to spend your Canada Day. On July 1st, you'll find a gigantic party on the lawns of Parliament Hill, at the Canadian Museum of History, and on downtown streets that are pedestrianised for the day.

(http://canadaday.gc.ca/eng/1399898650690)

18. Walk Through Four Ecosystems in the Montreal Biodome

Although Canada is a place that is well known for its incredible natural landscapes and outdoor attractions, there is only one place where you can walk around four different ecosystems in one day, and that's at the

Montreal Biodome in, you guessed it, Montreal. The four ecosystems are the ecosystems that you will find in the Americas, and comprise the tropical forest of South America, the Laurentian Forest of the North American Wilderness, the Saint Lawrence Marine Ecosystem, and a polar area as well.

(4777 Avenue Pierre-De Coubertin, Montréal, QC H1V 1B3, http://espacepourlavie.ca/en/biodome)

19. Have the Best BBQ of Your Life at Smoque N' Bones

Canada might not have a reputation as a gastronomic paradise, but foodies sure won't feel disappointed on their trip to this north American country. One of our favourite restaurants in Toronto, Smoque N' Bones specialises in two of life's greatest joys: barbecue and cocktails. The slow cooked meats are as moist and flavour filled as you are ever likely to taste, whether you go for chicken drumsticks, brisket, or ribs. And, of course, the cocktails wash everything down very nicely indeed.

(869 Queen St W, Toronto, ON M6J 1G4, http://smoquenbones.com/)

20. Sip on Beers at the Banff Craft Beer Festival

When you think of nations around the world that are particularly well known for their beers, somewhere like Germany or the Czech Republic might spring to mind. But you certainly don't have to miss out on the beer loving fun if you make it to the Banff Craft Beer Festival, which is hosted at the end of November each year. All of the beers on offer will be local, so it's a great opportunity to really sip on the taste of the Rockies.

21. Enjoy the Celebration of Light in Vancouver

Vancouver is a pretty quiet and relaxed place, but there is one time of the year when the city comes to life with colour, lights, and music, and that's at the end of July for the Celebration of Light. On the English Bay Beach, you'll find barges on the water from three countries, and each of these countries releases their most spectacular fireworks into the air. It's a great idea to bring a picnic and some blankets, and make a night of it on the beach.

(www.hondacelebrationoflight.com)

22. Take a Relaxing Sip in the Banff Hot Springs

The town of Banff in the Canadian Rockies is a place where people commonly go to enjoy adventure activities such as skiing, dog sledding, and skating. But if you feel like taking it easy, Banff also offers the perfect opportunity for relaxation with the Banff Hot Springs. While relaxing in the outdoor hot pool, it's possible to relax your weary muscles and take in an incredible view of Mount Rundle at the same time.

(1 Mountain Ave, Banff, AB T1L 1K2, www.hotsprings.ca)

23. Go Ice Skating in Nathan Phillips Square

Toronto is a city that is brimming full with public spaces, and Nathan Phillips Square is one of the main plazas in the city, located in front of Toronto City Hall. There are all kinds of public events here including concerts and markets, but we think the square is at its best in the winter months, when part of it gets transformed into a seasonal ice skating rink. It's a wonderful festive activity that the whole family can enjoy.

(100 Queen St W, Toronto, ON M5H 2N2)

24. Take a Pottery Class at the Gardiner Museum

If you are the kind of person who prefers to d things rather than walk around museums endlessly, the Gardiner Museum might just be the place to twist your arm. This ceramics museum does have an incredible display of international and historic ceramics work, but they also have pottery classes inside the museum if you fancy having a go on the potter's wheel and seeing if you could become a master ceramicist.

(111 Queens Park, Toronto, ON M5S 2C7, www.gardinermuseum.on.ca)

25. Swim in the 30 Foot Hole of Lynn Canyon Park

Vancouver is one of the sunniest and warmest places in Canada, and in the summer months the city's temperatures can ascend in rather an alarming way. Fortunately, there's a wonderful way to cool down, and that's by taking a plunge into the 30 foot hole of Lynn Canyon Park. Once inside the park, taking the trail will take you directly to the pool where you'll find local people enjoy the clean and cool waters.

(3663 Park Rd, North Vancouver, BC V7J 3G3, http://lynncanyon.ca)

26. Stroll the Alleys of Kensington Market

When you hear "Kensington Market", you could be forgiven for thinking that you would be visiting a market in the traditional sense, but Kensington Market is actually the name of a whole neighbourhood. With this said, the neighbourhood does have a bustling market feel with lots of quaint cafes and second hand shops, and so it's a place to walk around at leisure, pass some quiet hours, and perhaps pick up something special.

(Kensington Ave, Toronto, ON M5T 2K2, www.kensington-market.ca)

27. Ski the Canadian Rockies

For landscapes to die for combined with some of the most exciting outdoor adventures that you can possibly imagine, the Canadian Rockies is the destination for you. With numerous peaks and lots of snow, this is, of course, one of the most enduringly popular spots for a skiing adventure on the snow. There are plenty of ski resorts in the Rockies, but we are particularly enamoured by the Fernie Alpine Resort, which has 2500 metres of skiing terrain.

(5339 Fernie Ski Hill Rd, Fernie, BC V0B 1M6, www.skifernie.com)

28. Be Stunned by Montreal's Notre Dame Basilica

When it comes to church architecture in Canada, nothing can compare to the grandeur of the Notre Dame Basilica in Montreal. This Neo-Gothic church was designed in the early 19th century, and is large enough to hold 4000 people inside. There is a lot to attract the eyes inside the church. The interiors are grand and colourful, the ceiling is a beautiful deep blue colour with golden stars, and the stained glass windows depict scenes from the religious history of Montreal.

(110 Rue Notre-Dame O, Montréal, QC H2Y 1T, www.basiliquenddm.org/en/)

29. Go Back in Time at the Forks National Historic Site

When you're in Winnipeg, a must visit spot is the Forks National Historic site, a 9 acre park that has been designed to celebrate the 6000 year human history at the junction of the Red and Assiniboine Rivers. There is always something to do and explore in the park, no matter the time of year you visit. There are walking trails, there is a canoe beach that kids love, temporary exhibits, a native prairie garden, and even an amphitheatre where you can watch shows.

(Forks Market Rd, Winnipeg, MB R3C 4S8)

30. Enjoy a Little Shopping at Bonsecours Market

It goes without saying that before you leave this beautiful country, you will want to find some unique items that you can take home with you, and that will always remind you of Canada. We think that Bonsecours Market in Montreal is just the place. Located inside a 150 year old building, this indoor market contains many boutique shops, many of which are dedicated to local arts and crafts. So whether you would like to find a beautiful scarf, some silver jewellery, or anything else for that matter, you are sure to lay your hands on something special.

(350 Rue Saint Paul E, Montréal, QC H2Y 1H2, www.marchebonsecours.qc.ca/en)

31. Indulge a Sweet Tooth With a Nanaimo Bar

If you have a sweet tooth, there's one thing in Canada that we thing will please your stomach very much indeed, and that's the Nanaimo Bar. This is a bar dessert that requires no baking at all, and usually consists of a crumb based layer, topped by a custard flavoured butter icing, which is in turn topped by a layer of melted chocolate. It mixes smooth, crunchy, and sweet, and you can find these all over Canada.

32. Learn About Bugs at the Montreal Insectarium

So, we're guessing that you haven't made it all the way to Canada to get a schooling in insects, but if you do happen to be a fan of the outdoors and wildlife we think that the Montreal Insectarium might be a place for you to enjoy. It is the largest insect museum in North America, and one of the largest in the whole world, in fact. With 160,000 insects across more than 100 species, this place is sure to inspire and entertain.

(4581 Rue Sherbrooke E, Montréal, QC H1X 2B2, http://espacepourlavie.ca/en/insectarium)

33. Watch a Shakespeare Play in High Park

Every major city has its defining park. In London you'll find Hyde Park, in New York you can stroll the greenery of Central Park, and in Toronto you have High Park. And this is more than just a place to enjoy the outdoors, because every summer you can catch a series of outdoor Shakespeare performances right within the park. It's the perfect way of blending nature and culture on balmy Toronto evenings.

(1873 Bloor St W, Toronto, ON M6R 2Z3, www.highparktoronto.com)

34. Enjoy the Forest of Pacific Spirit Regional Park

If you find yourself in Vancouver, and you're looking for a way to escape city life for an afternoon, a trip to the Pacific Spirit Regional Park, which lies just west of the city would be an ideal place to hang out. With 73km of walking trails, this is a place where you can strap on your hiking boots and really feel immersed in the natural world. Most of the park is forest, but there is also a beach area where you can relax with a picnic.

(5495 Chancellor Blvd, Vancouver, BC V6T 1E4)

35. See the Stars at Rio Tinto Alcan Planetarium

The Rio Tino Alcan Planetarium is a fairly new addition to Montreal's learning scene, as this very interesting building only opened in 2013. With two full dome theatres, it's possible to get a comprehensive sense of the world that exists far beyond planet Earth. The exhibit on meteors is particularly good, as is the show that takes you on a journey through the Northern Lights.

(4801 Avenue Pierre-De Coubertin, Montréal, QC H1V 3N4)

36. Let Science World Capture Your Imagination

Travelling with kids can be rewarding, but there's no doubt that it's also a challenge. Somewhere that your kids can be entertained but also learn something is the Science World of Vancouver, which is, of course, a science museum, but it's not the least bit stuffy and places a huge focus on interactive learning. You and your children can put yourself to the test with mental puzzles that test your logic and creativity, and you can learn all about light, sound, and physics.

(1455 Quebec St, Vancouver, BC V6A 3Z7, www.scienceworld.ca)

37. Down a Bloody Caesar at the Westin Hotel in Calgary

If you think that a Bloody Mary is the perfect pick-me-up to down with Sunday brunch, you are going to fall head over heels for its Canadian sister cocktail, the Bloody Caesar. This cocktail contains the classic Bloody Mary ingredients of vodka, tomato juice, Worcestershire Sauce, and Tabasco sauce, but it also adds clam broth for an extra savoury element. This drink was actually invented in the Westin Hotel in Calgary, so be sure to try one while you're in town.

(320 4 Ave SW, Calgary, AB T2P 2S6, www.westincalgary.com)

38. See Magnificent Artworks at Vancouver's Anthropology Museum

You might think of an Anthropology Museum as a place to see dusty objects from the past, but at the Vancouver Anthropology Museum it's the artworks that really stand out, because it's here that you will find some of the finest examples of First Nations art, and in a spectacular building that overlooks the ocean. The guided tours are well worth splashing out for to get a more comprehensive understanding of the objects and art on display.

(6393 NW Marine Dr, Vancouver, BC V6T 1Z2, http://moa.ubc.ca)

39. Go White Water Rafting on the Horse Kicking River

The Rocky Mountains offer all kinds of outdoor adventures. The most obvious of these would be walking up mountains, but if you want to give your legs a rest, you can also take to the waters and enjoy the rapids of the Horse Kicking River. But although you won't be doing any exercise, don't expect this to be a smooth ride. The course runs for 22km, and the water is wild to say the least with class 3 and 4 rapids.

40. Taste the Sea at the BC Shellfish and Seafood Festival

British Columbia is totally covered by coastline on its western side, and this means it's a place where you can find some of the most epic seafood in all of Canada. The best place to sample as much of this deliciousness as possible is at the BC shellfish and seafood Festival. Celebrated every June, this festival gives visitors the opportunity to taste the wares of local shellfish farmers, and chow down on signature dishes from local seafood restaurants.

41. Stay in a Teepee in the Canadian Rockies

As you travel around Canada, you are likely to stay in hotels, hostels, and guesthouses, but if you fancy changing things up a bit, this country does have some stranger accommodation choices as well. At Goldenwood Lodge Teepess, located in the Canadian Rockies of British Columbia, you actually have the chance to stay in a teepee on the side of a river so you can feel totally in harmony with nature.

(2493 Holmes-Deakin Road, Golden, BC V0A 1H1, www.goldenwoodlodge.ca)

42. Have an Art Filled Day at the National Gallery of Canada

Located in Canada's capital city, Ottawa, the National Gallery of Canada is one of the premiere art spaces to be found in the country. And since the gallery opened in 1880, it's also a place that's historically important to Ottawa, and indeed Canada. Although the artworks inside are not exclusively Canadian, there is a strong focus on contemporary artists from Canada. Inside, you can also find some of Andy Warhol's most iconic works.

(380 Sussex Dr, Ottawa, ON K1N 9N4, www.gallery.ca/en/)

43. Indulge a Love of Wine at the Mission Hill Family Estate

When you think of places around the world that are famous for their wine production, California, France, or Argentina might spring to mind. While Canada might not be in the big leagues of wine production, there are still wineries dotted along the west coast that wine lovers might like to visit. One of the most pleasant of these is the Mission Hill Family Estate in the Okanagan Valley. The winery offers tours and tastings so you can get a real feel for this wine region.

(1730 Mission Hill Rd, West Kelowna, BC V4T 2E4, www.missionhillwinery.com)

44. Learn About the History of Shoes

Okay, we know that you haven't made it all the way to Canada to learn about shoes, but if you do happen to be in Toronto on a drizzly afternoon that calls for museum hopping, one of the most unique museums you can visit is the Bata Shoe Museum. This is the only museum in all of north America that is totally dedicated to footwear, and inside you can find more than 13,500 items from history and up to the present day. Important items include ballroom slippers worn by Queen Victoria and blue patent loafers that belonged to Elvis Presley.

(327 Bloor St W, Toronto, ON M5S 1W7, www.batashoemuseum.com)

45. Tuck Into Montreal Smoked Meat at Schwartz's Deli

Montreal might not be a place that stands out on the world's culinary map, but there are some local delicacies to try, and foodies will not be disappointed on a trip to this city. Something that all meat lovers should order is the Montreal smoked meat. This is a style of kosher deli meat that is produced by curing beef brisket with spices for a week, hot smoking it, and then steaming it. The most iconic spot for Montreal smoked meat in the city is as Schwartz's Deli, which dates all the way back to 1928.

(3895 Boul St-Laurent, Montréal, QC H2W 1X9, www.schwatrzsdeli.com)

46. Have a Dog Sledding Adventure in Banff

Many people enjoy the winter months of Canada to have adventures on the snow and ice that they wouldn't be able to have in their home countries. One of the most enduringly appealing of these adventures is dog sledding, and a popular place to do this is Banff. The wonderful thing about dog sledding is that you get to have an outdoor adventure and enjoy the Canadian landscapes without needing to be sporty at all. The dogs will pull you along, and you can simply enjoy the ride.

47. Take a Walk Around Beautiful Lake Louise

For total peace and quiet, and landscapes that will take your breath away, a trip to stunning Lake Louise in Banff National Park is a must. The best way to explore this hamlet is to use the well marked hiking trails. Depending on your fitness ability, you might want to take relaxed walks around the lake itself, or you can start at the lake and walk uphill, and from this vantage point you'll have an incredible view of the whole city.

48. Escape City Life at the Allan Gardens Conservatory

If you find yourself in Toronto and a little overwhelmed by city life, a great place to visit, and where you might forget you are inside a city altogether, is the Allan Gardens Conservatory. This garden filled greenhouse covers an area of over 16,000 square feet, and is more than a century old. Inside you will find plants from all over world including cactus plants, palm trees, tropical orchids, bamboo, and more besides.

(Allan Gardens Children's Conservatory, 19 Horticultural Ave, Toronto, ON M5A 2P2)

49. Eat Beachfront Seafood at Point Prim Chowder House

With so much coastline, Canada is a country that can offer some truly delicious seafood, and one of the best seafood restaurants in the whole country has to be Pint Prim Chowder House, which is located on the picturesque and peaceful Prince Edward Island. This place has incredible sunset views across the ocean, and offers the best of East Coast seafood fare such as steamed clam and mussels, fresh oysters, and a selection of delicious chowders.

(2150 Point Prim Rd, Belfast, PE C0A 1A0, www.chowderhousepei.com)

50. Take a Break in the Miette Hot Springs

The Canadian Rockies is the ultimate place for adventure travellers. You can climb up vertical mountain faces with cables, you can ski down step mountain slopes, and lots more besides. But after all that exertion, you'll want the chance to relax, and the Miette Hot Springs is the ideal spot to do exactly that. These are the warmest springs in the Rockies with temperatures of a comfortable 40 degrees Celsius. There are also minerals in the water to help you relax even further.

(www.hotsprings.ca/miette-hot-springs)

51. Enjoy an Outdoor Electronica Party, Piknic Elecktronik

If you are somebody who can't get enough of the atmosphere and fun of summer festivals, you will absolutely love Montreal's Piknic Electrnonika, because it is actually hosted on every single weekend of the summer. The festival definitely has a dance feel, with an emphasis placed on house and minimal techno, so if you love to dance to beats until the sun comes up, this is definitely the place for you to be.

(https://piknicelectronik.com/montreal/)

52. Step Back in Time at Black Creek Pioneer Village

If you are the kind of person who gets bored walking around the aisles of stuffy museums, the Black Creek Pioneer Village might be a place that is more to your liking. This is an open air heritage museum where you can actually walk around a historic village and see how life was in times past in a far more real way than if you were to simply view objects behind a glass screen. The village contains over forty 19th century buildings, including a farm building, a water powered mill, and a schoolhouse.

(1000 Murray Ross Pkwy, North York, ON M3J 2P3, www.blackcreek.ca)

53. Be Blown Away by Niagara Falls

Niagara Falls might just be the most iconic tourist spot in all of Canada, and it's with good reason. While there are actually more than 500 waterfalls in the world bigger than the Horseshoe Falls of Niagara Falls, there is no other waterfall that has such a surge of water, 750,000 gallons each second in fact, and it's the power of the mighty waterfall that makes it such a spectacle. A trip to Canada wouldn't be complete without feeling its spray on your skin.

54. Explore the Underwater Shipwrecks of Brockville

Brockville is a small city that lies in the eastern part of Canada in Ontario, and it's one of the foremost places in the world to have a freshwater scuba diving adventure. This means that you certainly won't see things like tropical fish or coral reefs, but what you will find are underwater shipwrecks, of which there are very many. There are many tour companies dotted around the city that can help you with your diving experience.

55. Watch a Gridiron Football Game at Montreal Olympic Stadium

Gridiron football, otherwise known as American football, might not be quite as popular as the national sport of ice hockey, but it's still big news in Canada, and if you are the sporty type, it can be a great idea to catch a game. Of course, you'll find local matches in stadiums all over the country, but one stadium where the spectator experience is unrivalled is the Montreal Olympic Stadium. The stadium was built specifically for the 1976 Olympics, and has capacity to hold more than 66,000 football fans.

(4141 Avenue Pierre-De Coubertin, Montréal, QC H1V 3N7, http://parcolympique.qc.ca/en/the-park/olympic-stadium/)

56. Wave a Rainbow Flag at Pride Toronto

Canada has a reputation of being a very tolerant nation, and as you can imagine, this means that the LGBT population can live very safely in the country. This also means that the Pride celebrations around the country are very visible, and that they are a hell of a lot of fun to join in with. The biggest of the celebrations is at Pride Toronto, which takes place each year at the end of June. The festivities culminate in a huge street parade, with plenty of music, colour, and dancing.

(www.pridetoronto.com)

57. Go Salmon Fishing Along the Miramichi

If your idea of a perfect getaway involves sitting on the banks of a river with your fishing rod in the water, you are in luck because there are plenty of awesome fishing destinations all over the country. This is one of the premiere rivers in the whole world for finding large populations of Atlantic Wild Salmon. While some areas are private, there's also plenty of public fishing pools where you can sit and fish all day to your heart's content.

58. Discover Local History at the Ramparts of Quebec City

Quebec City is a special place for a whole range of reasons, and not least because it's North America's one and only remaining fortified city, and it is possible to tour and explore these fortifications otherwise known as the Ramparts of Quebec City. As you walk along the ramparts, you will discover three centuries of history in this part of Quebec and you'll have fantastic cityscapes of the whole city.

(2 Rue d'Auteuil, Ville de Québec, QC G1R 5C2)

59. Say Hi to the Animals at Toronto Zoo

If you are an animal lover, deciding whether to visit a zoo or not can be difficult. Not all zoos have ethical practices, but the good news is that Toronto Zoo is dedicated to breeding endangered species such as the Blanding's turtle. Toronto Zoo also happens to be the largest zoo in all of Canada, and with over 450 animal species inside the park, there's no chance of getting bored. Some of the animals you'll have the chance to see include Indian rhinos, Sumatran tigers, and a giant Pacific octopus.

(2000 Meadowvale Rd, Toronto, ON M1B 5K7, www.torontozoo.com)

60. Stroll Through the Gardens of Queen Elizabeth Park

Vancouver has always held the reputation of being Canada's green city. And when you take a stroll through Queen Elizabeth Park you will understand why. This 130 acre park contains a floral conservatory, quarry gardens, an arboretum, a sculpture gardens, and some beautiful fountains and pavilions. It's also located at one of the highest points of the city, so as you stroll you'll have a great view of the rest of city and mountains in the distance.

(4600 Cambie St, Vancouver, BC V5Y 2M9, http://vancouver.ca/parks-recreation-culture/queen-elizabeth-park.aspx)

61. Have a Bobsleigh Adventure in Canada Olympic Park

If you are the sporty type, you need to etch a trip to the Canada Olympic Park in Calgary on your Canada must visit list. This park is actually a place where professional athletes train for all kinds of winter sporting activities, but you don't have to be a pro to make use of the facilities, many of which are also open to the public. One of the most thrilling activities you can enjoy is a bobsleigh ride, which involves being piloted around a course and experiencing speeds of 80km/hour.

(88 Canada Olympic Rd SW, Calgary, AB T3B 5R5, www.winsport.ca/)

62. See Beluga Whales off the Coast of Churchill

Beluga whales are some of the most beautiful looking creatures on this planet, and they are gargantuan in size with bodies that can extend for 18 feet, and with a weight that can reach 1600 kilograms. They also happen to live in the coastline just off Churchill, a town in Manitoba. There are tour companies that can take you out on their boats so that you can actually see these sea mammals up close, which is sure to be a once in a lifetime experience.

63. Try Delicious Quebec Cheeses at La Fromagerie Atwater

Thanks to the French influence in Canada, it is possible to chow down on all kinds of delicious and stinky cheeses in the country, especially when you are in the French speaking part of Canada. If you are a cheese lover who finds themselves in Montreal, La Fromagerie Atwater is a place that you 100% need to visit. This family business has a huge selection of Quebec cheeses so that you can really enjoy the local taste on your visit.

(Atwater Market, 134 Atwater Ave, Montréal, www.fromagerieatwater.ca/en)

64. Step Back in Time at the Ukrainian Cultural Heritage Village

Canada has earned a reputation as a country that is very welcoming to foreigners who wish to settle in the country, and actually, this is no recent phenomenon. Between the years of 1899 and 1930 there were tonnes of Ukrainian settlers in the Alberta area, and you can learn more about this in the Ukrainian Cultural Heritage Village, an open-air museum where learning is always fun. The village contains farmsteads with farm machinery, typical homes, and actors who remain in character throughout.

(Hwy 16 E, Tofield, AB T0B 4J0, www.history.alberta.ca/ukrainianvillage)

65. Get Stuck Into Local History at Pointe-a-Calliere Museum

Montreal is a city with one of the most fascinating histories in all of North America, and the best place to learn about local history is at the Pointe-a-Calliere Museum. Inside the museum, you'll find archaeological objects from every period in the city's history, and it has one of the largest archaeological collections in Canada. There is also a strong emphasis on how Britain and France influenced this Canadian region in the past.

(350 Place Royale, Montréal, QC H2Y 3Y5, https://pacmusee.qc.ca/en/)

66. Enjoy the Music at Winnipeg Folk Festival

If you would like to experience the fun of a summer music festival, but you don't fancy all night partying, we think that the Winnipeg Folk Festival, which is hosted every second weekend of July, could be just the ticket for you. Over 80,000 people join in with the festivities to hear the smooth sounds of folk over the weekend, and you can hear all kinds of folk music including bluegrass, Celtic, indie folk, Americana, and more.

(www.winnipegfolkfestival.ca)

67. Treat Yourself to a BeaverTails Pastry

When you think of food to eat in Canada, you probably first think of poutine, and then you might get stuck. But those with a sweet tooth will not be left out on a trip to this country, and one of the best sweet treats that Canada has to offer is called a BeaverTail. The reason for the name is that the pastry is hand stretched to resemble a beaver's tail. It is then covered with ingredients like whipped cream, crumbled cookies, sprinkles, and other treats.

(www.beavertails.com)

68. Visit the Museum of Vancouver, Canada's Largest Civic Museum

Museum lovers will be enamoured on a trip to Vancouver, because this charming Canadian city contains the country's largest civic museum, the Museum of Vancouver. This museum dates all the way back to 1984, so as you can imagine, there are many objects that have been collected since then. Inside you'll find everything from hand written letters by Vancouver residents exploring the British Empire, to household objects from the city's history.

(1100 Chestnut St, Vancouver, BC V6J 3J9, www.museumofvancouver.ca)

69. Take in the Incredible Views From Lions Gate Bridge

Vancouver is most certainly a city of bridges, and there's more than a handful of bridges that you can walk across. One of our favourites is the Lions Gate Bridge. This suspension bridge is very impressive with an expanse of 1823 metres, crossing the Burrard Inlet. Although this is principally a bridge that carries vehicles, pedestrians also have their own their own footpath, and the views from the centre of the bridge are nothing short of breath taking.

70. Have the Best Winter Ever at the SnowKing Winter Festival

Winter time is a wonderful time of year to visit Canada, but if you don't fancy the usual activities like skiing and skating, something alternative that might grab your attention is the SnowKing Winter Festival, which is held in Yellowknife in the Northwest Territories in March. The whole festival is built in a snow castle built from snow and ice. At the festival, films are projected directly on to the snow walls, plays are staged, there are music concerts, and lots more fun besides.

(www.snowking.ca)

71. Discover an Incredible Art Collection at Art Gallery of Ontario

When you think of artsy countries around the world, Canada might not be the first country that springs to mind, but actually the cities in Canada host some of the finest galleries in north America. The Art Gallery of Ontario, which you can find in Toronto, is one of these. Inside, you will find more than 80,000 artworks that extend from the 1st century right up to the present day. Highlights include the incredible collection of Canadian art and the Henry Moore Sculpture Centre.

(317 Dundas St W, Toronto, ON M5T 1G4, www.ago.net)

72. Visit a Japanese Teahouse in Nitobe Memorial Garden

After a hectic morning of sightseeing, one of the nicest things that you can do is relax with a refreshing cup of green tea, and there is no place more atmospheric to sip on tea than in the teahouse at Nitobe Memorial Garden in Vancouver. This is one of the most authentic Japanese gardens in all of North America, and in the teahouse you can experience a Japanese tea ceremony just as you would in Kyoto.

(1895 Lower Mall, Vancouver, BC V6T 1Z4, http://botanicalgarden.ubc.ca/visit/nitobe-memorial-garden/)

73. Take in a Show at the Toronto Fringe Festival

Toronto is a city in Canada with an incredible creative buzz, and you can really experience the creative energy of this city if you find yourself in this part of the world during July when the Toronto Fringe Festival takes place. During this festival, you can normally see over 150 shows in 25 venues around the city, and whether you prefer stand-up comedy, physical theatre, or straight plays, there will be something for you.

(www.fringetoronto.com/fringe-festival/)

74. Eat Traditional Quebecois Cuisine at La Binerie Mont-Royal

Canada is a huge country, and this means that you can expect to eat different types of food as you travel around the country. Because of the French and British influence, the food you will find in the Quebec region is often quite different to the food in other parts of the country, and one of our favourite Quebecois restaurants is La Binerie Mont-Royal in Montreal. Things like traditional baked beans, pea soup, and spruce beer are on offer.

(367 Avenue du Mont-Royal E, Montréal, QC H2T 1R1, www.labineriemontroyal.com)

75. Learn About Canada's Agricultural History at the Ross Farm Museum

The province of Nova Scotia contains 3795 farms that produce many things such as barley, fruits, vegetables, and livestock. If you would like to know more about this aspect of life in the country, be sure to visit the Ross Farm Museum. This agricultural museum gives visitors an understanding of the region's rural heritage with historic farm buildings, antique farming implements, and working artisans.

(4568 Highway #12, New Ross, NS B0J 2M0, https://rossfarm.novascotia.ca)

76. Explore the Natural World at the Canadian Museum of Nature

If you are a nature lover, you probably think that the best way to experience the nature of Canada is to actually get outdoors. There is undoubtedly a lot of truth to this, but we also have the recommend the Canadian Museum of Nature in Ottawa. This museum of natural history has many things to inspire. As you walk around the aisles, you can find a fossil gallery containing dinosaur fossils, a mammals gallery with mountings of grizzly bears, and lots more besides.

(240 McLeod St, Ottawa, ON K2P 2R1, www.nature.ca/en)

77. Walk Across the Capilano Suspension Bridge

Vancouver is one of those cities with plenty to enjoy on the outskirts of the city, and so you shouldn't just limit your time in Vancouver to the city centre. In the northern part of the district, something that nature and adventure lovers won't want to miss is the Capilano Suspension Bridge, a bridge that is 70 metres high, 140 metres long, and assists visitors in crossing the Capilano River. From there, you'll have a magnificent view of the nature around you – perfect for holiday snaps and selfies.

(3735 Capilano Rd, North Vancouver, BC V7R 4J1, www.capbridge.com)

78. Enjoy a Typical Canadian Dessert, Butter Tart

If you find yourself in Canada during the winter time, and you can stand to take in a few extra calories to keep yourself warm, waste no time and get a delicious butter tart inside of you. This is one of Canada's staple treats and although it's simple, it's very delicious. A flaky pastry tart case is simply filled with a sweet egg custard so that it becomes semi-firm, and that's the extent of it. You'll also find some bakers who create different flavour custards, such as pumpkin or maple bacon.

79. Be Mesmerised by the Northern Lights at Hudson Bay

The upper reaches of the northern hemisphere are famous for one very spectacular natural phenomenon: the Northern Lights. The Northern Lights occur when electrically charged particles enter the earth's atmosphere above the magnetic poles, and the particles show visibly as swathes of beautiful auroral light, normally in green and pink colours. It is possible to see this natural display for yourself at Hudson Bay, and there are a few tour companies that can take you to see nature's light show at optimal places with comfortable viewing points.

80. Go Bird Watching in Point Pelee National Park

Canada is a country that is bursting full with all kinds of exciting life. Of course, there are things like deer and moose and bears, but you are missing a whole part of the Canadian ecosystem if you fail to look to the skies because there are parts of Canada that are extremely rich in bird life. Pint Pelee Park, which you can find in the south-eastern state of Ontario is one such place. In fact, 370 species of birds have been recorded here, so be sure to have your binoculars ready.

(1118 Point Pelee Dr, Leamington, ON N8H 3V4, www.pc.gc.ca/eng/pn-np/on/pelee/index.aspx)

81. Sip on Creative Cocktails at Black Hoof Cocktail Bar

There is plenty to amuse yourself with on a Friday night in cocktail, but if you've just spent a long day sightseeing, all you might be able to manage is a couple of decadent cocktails, and the place for some of the best cocktails in the city is The Black Hoof. Whether you want a classic or something different, the mixologists have something up their sleeve. We are very fond of the Mescalero, which combines cardamom tequila, mezcal, aperol, grapefruit liqueur and egg white.

(928 Dundas St W, Toronto, ON M6J 1W, www.theblackhoof.com)

82. Explore the Joggins Fossil Cliffs

If you would like to see natural history, right there in front of you, you can skip the museums around the country, and head to the Joggins Fossil Cliffs in Nova Scotia instead. It's here that you can find fossils from a rainforest ecosystem that dates back an astonishing 310 million years ago. Many discoveries have been made here, including the earliest ever known reptile, many early amphibian species, members of the calamites family, and lots more besides.

(100 Main St, Joggins, NS B0L 1A0, www.jogginsfossilcliffs.net/)

83. Get Back to Nature in Edwards Gardens

While Toronto is the most populated city in Canada, it's still not too overwhelming, with just over 2 million people living there. And with so many green spaces, if you do feel a little overwhelmed by people and traffic, there are plenty of places to get back to nature within the city itself. One of these places is called Edwards Gardens, which are botanical gardens with roses, wildflowers, and a rockery.

(755 Lawrence Ave E, North York, ON M3C 1P2)

84. Take in a Show at the Royal Alexandra Theatre

Built way back in 1907, the Royal Alexandra Theatre in Toronto is actually the oldest theatre in North America that is still operational today. This gorgeous beaux-arts style theatre has two balconies, can seat 1497 people, and was built in the way of traditional British theatres of the 19th century. Over the years, the stage has attracted many acclaimed performers such as Lucille Ball, Maggie Smith, and Ingrid Bergman. Keep up with their schedule of events to see a show yourself.

(260 King St W, Toronto, ON M5V 1H9, http://www.mirvish.com/theatres/royal-alexandra-theatre)

85. Fill Your Stomach at Winnipeg's Forks Market

One of the highlights of any trip to Winnipeg has to be a visit to the Forks Market, which combines two of life's greatest joys: eating and shopping. In the early 1900s, the Forks Market was originally two horse stables, and these were eventually connected by a courtyard to create the ultimate market destination in the city. In the food emporium, you'll find everything from local cheese to amazing wines, and there are also boutique shops and stalls selling things like leather goods, ceramics, cigars, and more.

(1 Forks Market Rd, Winnipeg, MB R3C 4L9, www.theforks.com/attractions/at-the-forks/the-forks-market)

86. Look Out For Bears in Jasper National Park

Covering a staggering 4200 square miles, Jasper National Park is the largest national park in the Canadian Rockies, with plenty to explore. This natural wilderness if jammed full with incredible mammals such as mountain goats, elk, moose, coyotes, and cougars, but there's really just one animal that people home to see: the bears. Black bear mother and cub sightings are fairly common, and generally don't pose a threat.

(www.pc.gc.ca/eng/pn-np/ab/jasper/index.aspx)

87. Take a Guided Tour of Ottawa's Parliament Buildings

If you have any interest in history and politics, the Parliament Buildings of Canada, which can be found in Ottawa, are well worth a visit. Set on a dramatic hill overlooking the Ottawa River, and consist of gorgeous Gothic style buildings that date way back to the mid 19th century. It is possible to enjoy a free guided tour of the parliament buildings every day, the highlight of which is making your way to the top of the peace building where you have a wonderful view of the whole city.

(Wellington St, Ottawa, ON K1A 0A4)

88. Pick Your Own Lobster at Hall's Harbour Lobster Pond

When it comes to luxurious dinners, it doesn't get more decadent than chowing down on a freshly cooked lobster, and in our opinion the best place for a lobster dinner in all of Canada is at Hall's Harbour Lobster

Pond in Centreville, Nova Scotia. This fishing village dates all the way back to 1779, so you know the catch is going to be good quality, and you can even pick your own lobster from their lobster pond.

(1157 W Halls Harbour Rd, Centreville, NS B0P 1J0, www.hallsharbourlobster.com)

89. Discover Aquatic Life at Vancouver Aquarium

Vancouver is a city right on the west coast of Canada, and there's all kinds of marine life to be found in its waters. If you don't fancy getting your feet wet, you can still get up close to the aquatic life of Vancouver by visiting the Vancouver Aquarium, which contains 70,000 sea animals. Highlights in the aquarium include blacktip reef sharks, green sea turtles, and octopuses.

(845 Avison Way, Vancouver, BC V6G 3E2, www.vanaqua.org)

90. Celebrate the Winter Months at Ottawa's Winterlude

In some countries, you might want to avoid winter weather at all costs, but when you're in Canada, the winter time is a cause for celebration, and this is never more evident than at Ottawa's annual Winterlude festival. The festival takes place across three weekends in February, and attracts hundreds of thousands of visitors every year. The focal point of the festival is the Rideau Canal Skateway, which is actually the largest skating rink in the whole world.

91. Have a Climbing Adventure to Longs Peak

Canada is an adventure lover's dream destination, with varied landscapes that lend themselves to many kinds of outdoor activities. If it's climbing up mountains that gets you going, we can heartily recommend, climbing your ay up Longs Peak, a prominent summit among the famous Rocky Mountains. The mountain ascends to a peak of 4346 metres, and the climb is not for the faint hearted. You will need some prior climbing experience as you'll need to ascend with cables for part of the climb.

92. Stroll Through Canada's Foremost Castle, Casa Loma

North America doesn't have too many castles, but quite unbelievably, you can actually find one in Toronto city. Unlike some other castles, this building doesn't have a grand history of defending its city, but was actually built in the early 20th century by a wealthy financier. Nowadays, the castle and grounds are owned by the city, and its possible for visitors to explore its grand towers, spiralling staircases, stables, and five acre gardens.

(1 Austin Terrace, Toronto, ON M5R 1X8, www.casaloma.ca)

93. Take in Some Smooth Sounds at Montreal Jazz Fest

If you love nothing more than to hear the smooth sounds of jazz music, you need to know about the Montreal Jazz Fest, which takes place at the end of June and beginning of July each year. Since this festival actually holds the record of being the largest jazz festival in the world, it's truly a must visit for jazz aficionados. The festival has previously hosted jazz icons like John Lee Hooker, Muddy Waters, and Ray Charles.

(http://www.montrealjazzfest.com/default-en.aspx)

94. Celebrate Celtic Culture at Celtic Colours International Festival

More than nine million Canadians, which is a quarter of the population, can claim to have Scottish or Irish heritage, which means that the Celtic influence upon Canada should not be underestimated. A place where this heritage is celebrated is the Celtic Colours International Festival, which is hosted on Cape Breton island in October every year. You can expect musicians, singing, dancing, handicrafts, storytelling, and lots more fun besides.

(www.celtic-colours.com)

95. Hit a Few Golf Balls on Cape Breton Island

With so much green space across Canada, it should come as no surprise to learn that this country has more than a handful of awesome golf courses. The best of them all is a strong matter of debate, but we like Cabot Links on Cape Breton Island very much. This golf course is special because six of the eighteen holes are played directly on the ocean, and each of these offers incredible ocean vistas.

(15933 Central Ave, Inverness, NS B0E 1N0, www.cabotlinks.com)

96. Get Artsy at the Montreal Museum of Fine Arts

If you are a museum and gallery fanatic, you cannot leave Montreal before spending at least an afternoon at the Montreal Museum of Fine Arts, which is the largest museum in the whole of the city, with a very impressive art collection indeed. In fact, with 42000 works of art in the museum, it's more than possible to spend a few days walking the gallery's aisles. Notable artists on display include Rembrandt and Rubens.

(1380 Rue Sherbrooke O, Montréal, QC H3G 1J5, http://www.mbam.qc.ca/en)

97. Enjoy Food, Fire, and Music at The Gathering

Newfoundland exists in the most eastern part of the country, but it's well worth trekking there to attend The Gathering, a celebration of food, fire, and music, which is hosted at the end of August each year in Burlington. This is a back to nature and back to basics experience with hunks of meat that are grilled on bear flames and acoustic performances around the campfire.

(www.thegatheringburlington.com)

98. Keep Kids Happy at the Ontario Science Centre

Travelling with kids is no easy task. While you want to provide them with great memories that they can look back on, keeping kids entertained around the clock is easier said than done. One place where kids will be entertained and where they can learn something is the Ontario Science Centre in Toronto. This is not like an ordinary stuffy museum, because almost everything inside is interactive. Once inside, you'll have the opportunity to pilot a rocket, touch a tornado, grapple with a climbing wall, and lots more.

(770 Don Mills Rd, North York, ON M3C 1T3, www.ontariosciencecentre.ca)

99. Hike to the Della Falls

There are many waterfalls dotted around Canada, but of course, there's only one that can be considered the tallest, and that is Della Falls, which is located on Vancouver Island. With a total vertical drop of 440 metres, this waterfall is truly spectacular, and it's actually possible to hike to the waterfall if you would like to see it yourself. Located in Strathcona Provincial Park, there is a 15km trail that will take you right to the base of the falls.

100. Tuck Into Peameal Bacon Sandwiches

Meat lovers should be prepared to feast on their trip to Canada, because this country has some delicious cuts, and one of our favourites has to be peameal bacon, which is really quite different from the bacon most people are used to. This is a variety of back bacon from boneless pork loin that is wet cured, and then rolled in cornmeal. In Toronto, this bacon is often put between slices of fluffy bread with some slice tomato and a fried egg, and eaten as an on-the-go lunch.

101. Spend the Night in a Former Jail

Booking hostel accommodation is a great way of meeting other travellers like you and finding people to hang out with on your trips around Canada, but not all hostels are built equal, and one of the most unique hostels in the whole country is the Ottawa Jail Hostel. This building was originally the Carleton County Gaol, and when the jail closed in 1972 it became a hostel, but still features many of its original features so a stay there kinda feels like spending the night in prison.

(75 Nicholas St, Ottawa, ON K1N 7B9)

Before You Go...

Thanks for reading **101 Coolest Things to Do in Canada.** We hope that it makes your trip a memorable one!

Keep your eyes peeled on www.101coolestthings.com, and have a wonderful time in Canada!

Team 101 Coolest Things

Printed in Germany
by Amazon Distribution
GmbH, Leipzig